BORDER CROSSINGS

poems by

Raymond Berthelot

Finishing Line Press
Georgetown, Kentucky

BORDER CROSSINGS

ACKNOWLEDGMENTS

Grateful acknowledgement is due to the editors of the following journals, in
which these poems first appeared:

The Elevation Review: "Another Poem by the Sea"
Apricity Magazine: "Pastoral Heaven"
Peregrine Journal: "Communication Paradox"
Mantis: A Journal of Poetry: "A Long Way from Home," "Street Light,"
     "Sunset"
Progenitor Art & Literary Journal: "The Border Crossing"
The Bluebird Word: "What They Can't Take Away"
Lothlorien Poetry Journal: "Le Old Navy," "Flower Water," "That Town Best,"
     "Impressionist"

"Birds, Saints and Wet Markets" was incorporated into an art instillation by
Ron Bennett at the Second Story Gallery, New Orleans, January 9th, 2021
through February 6th, 2021.

Publisher: Leah Huete de Maines
Editor: Christen Kincaid
Cover Art: "Autumn moon over Tama River" The New York Public Library
Digital Collections. 1838
Author Photo: Gerardina Berthelot
Cover Design: Elizabeth Maines McCleavy

Order online: www.finishinglinepress.com
          also available on amazon.com

Author inquiries and mail orders:
Finishing Line Press
PO Box 1626
Georgetown, Kentucky 40324
USA

Contents

for Oriana Marie, with love

Cold War Ghazal

Grey is blue wanting to be black
like a cold war European city on ice

Madonna is youth, MTV in color
and the Poles get this

We have missiles, they have some too
while the music tells us to stop, dance

Dublin and Vienna are the new capitols
we've left DC to the great actors of our age

We've tried to give peace a chance for almost twenty years now
to no avail

No one can quench the thirst for fire in the jungles of Latin America
the poor in priestly collars try, to no avail

I've got a crush on youth
and so, there's still hope

Mocking Lorca

One lily in the valley
but not a lily of the valley
per se
opened one petal
maybe two
revealing one's pink orchid
yawning to receive honey dew
newly arrived from the moon
on the 3 am train
and I sighed at dawn
realizing that Venus
has stolen and scattered your petals
in the fields of morning

Another Poem by the Sea

Cool, clear morning on the Gulf
gentle roar comes in waves

Seagulls huddle
and one boat fishing reflects morning light

We witnessed a true feeding frenzy yesterday
dolphins and sharks together in ecstasy

Guests, debates, wine
early morning walks

A storm is forming dark along the horizon
sure to be moving towards us

A Long Way from Home

I pass two cowboys
standing next to their truck
on the side of the road, hood up
dust, grime
I do not stop.

I have a long way to go
and there is nothing,
I mean nothing
but fence, land, mountains
and the distance.

A dot moving on a very long, straight line
Only more land,
between here and there.

It sucks for them
but I drive on
somewhere between here and there
and offer a small prayer.

May help find its way
towards two rough cowboys
a broken truck
on the side of the road
a long
very long
road.

Theirs is not our Paris
(for Dina)

Our Paris is not like theirs, 'mor
holding hands, we walk along Rue Payenne
tired in the twilight, along by the archives
and Le Sévigné is too romantic for us tonight

We'll pass Musées and dine outside
at Petites Canailles
or steaks at the café across the street, on the corner

Marie Antoinette in the gardens
of the Hotel de Sully
might meet us afterwards
at Club Zero Zero

And perhaps we'll see that guy again
you know the one I mean
the one with the splendid hair

Birds, Saints and Wet Markets

Drip drip pink on the wet concrete floor
in the early morning Asiatic sun
like flowers erupting in oil
the butcher's blade
insatiably hungry
for the sacrificial soul
touch the sweet spot delicate
of another martyr
for man must eat
or surely
as surely as anything ever lived
man will die
and ascend upon a breeze of blues
silhouetted
against the early morning
Asiatic sun

In Memoriam
(for my father)

Wet and grey
as if the sun has been banished

Cold, clear crisp tomorrow
tomorrow

The first fire of the season
gumbo in the old pot on the stove, oysters waiting to be shucked
    outside

Like the spaces between the stars, memories
nothing stretching towards infinity

Upon the approaching front rides the past
while purple martins claim their territory

And we, alone
feel the absence deep within our bones

The New South

The gallery to myself
color prints of the new south
Confederate flags
racial harmony and segregation
poverty, industry at the expense of nature
obligatory hunting and fishing rights of passage
Civil War again and again
baptism in the blood of the lamb
like an early R.E.M. video
not that it's bad
it's just that it's not new
are we forever cursed
as our ancestors before us
to live in the new south

Together, alone

The guests left us
with lobster rolls and rain

We settled for wine
after a grey sunset

Pizza on the bed
and the constant, never ending roar of waves outside

Early morning, red in the east
to find not much has changed

A niece calls from France
to report more quarantining on the way

An Irish Dream

Sunlight through shuttered windowpanes
patterns on the wooden floor
while dust particles hang, hang suspended in air
smells like comfort and coffee
whiskey by the fire in the pub
like green hills and sheep in the salt air
outside, where they don't have to be seen
to be felt
like the sea
the distant sea
that will wait
there in the distance
waiting
warm and consoling
waiting
for me
alone

Street Light

One street light
yellow like the lollipop
in your hand
while sitting on the park bench
sunflower summer dress
cool in the heat of pigeons
looking for something something
anything to satiate this eternal hunger
that we all share
day after long day
by the light of the lamp
that turns us towards the morrow
and I must go now
really, I must go
bye now
bye

Pastoral Heaven

Their blood runs through me, now
those men and women whose blistered hands
plowed fields with mules and sweat
and still owe more to the company store
than to God.

Hard, callous souls
and thin sheets to keep off the croup,
hungry children,
hungrier than those buried at the church
up the dirt road.

This land is your land
this land is not our land
for he lives even further on up the road
yet close enough for us to feel his want

Sugar cane, cotton
beans and greens
don't amount to much this year
so we best gotta move on

Gotta move on
move on
so that their blood can flow
on and on
through me
now.

That Town Best

I like that town best
in the very early morning rain
cobble stones newly wet
mist blankets the cathedral and plaza

The dark smell of coffee
and a hint of last night's liquor
remind us that we're here now
but only passing through

The gypsy lady and the carnival juggler
declare their place in the square
and Calliope sings her song
to the rising sun

As she opens her eyes
weary, the smells of night love
still linger
as she reveals a suggestion
of somnolent contentment
and asks
to sleep for ten minutes more

Euphoria

I was given the six pills
and reminded
be mindful of alcohol

so I popped all six
with a beer
and now the world is oh so sharp

clear and in focus
almost beautiful
but from somewhere deep
I know

this world was never this
and I must get back
later though
not now
later

Melancholy Ghazal

The railroad bridge stands erect over the canal
as it always has for as long as I've known

Sky grey and low
wet and Spring's still further down the dirt road

The old man has no one left
so he searches out relatives he's never met

Shotgun houses still look like
the warmth of home from long ago

Some smells bring you back
further than others

We gather as friends
some of us are absent still

The blond at the bar in the yellow dress and black hat
tells me that Spring is just down the dirt road, and never looks
    my way

Dead Reckoning

The line, ever so thin line in the distance
      is the horizon

We drift towards the future, unaware
      wind at our backs

Alone on the sea, we've left hope far behind
      abandoned by all the former gods

Faith in birds never waivers
      they have proven to our grandfathers that they know the way

Stars at night offer slight comfort
      as the dark's wet breath whispers to our ears, alone, alone

No more need of your compass nor your sextant
      we continuously move, without

Beneath the horizon, towards an unseen, unknown point
      that from which we came, home

What They Can't Take Away

The sailboats at anchor
      are pulled in one direction
            by the tide between the keys

Remember that woman
      crazy or drunk, walking by the sanitarium
            she too, refused assistance

What is it about moonlight and tropical flowers?
      for a while at least
            peace seems possible

But back to the sea
      and the sun distantly setting, swollen
            at a place we'll never be

Fluid

She is fluid
and still
in control
drink tickets received
and magic created
into the night
the light here
dim, radiant
skin, hair
glow
as she is
now
her eyes
mine
lock
momentarily
wet, deep
as if to say
I'm so tired
of the bullshit
you wouldn't even
begin
to understand

Communication Paradox

A certain species of bird
        now almost extinct
        is reportedly losing its language
        meanwhile scientists, no doubt well meaning
        in their white lab coats
        have developed a method
        to give these birds, their language back
        I fear though
        we do not yet know
        by what name they call themselves

My dog, Luna Rose
        not yet two
        has learned when to wake me in the morning
        so that I can prepare her breakfast
        the way she likes
        and my dear wife
        now married to me almost thirty years
        still claims to not know
        what the hell I'm trying to say

We've only recently learned
        that the names by which
        we call certain tribes
        are for the most part
        from the language of enemies
        translated to mean
        "the child eaters over the hill"

Communication seems to be a lost skill
        amongst us
        I'm certain though
        the birds have a word
        for what I'm trying to say
        in their language

A Buddhist Poem, as if

I push at the skin of the universe
thump the rind and listen for morality echoes
sounds sweet, as if possible
I'll take anyway
ripe, summer day, picnic
we leave for the meadow, for the stream
looking forward
to when nature's senses
drip down my chin
and I spit out the seeds
of this material world

A Feather

There is a feather
tiny, faded with a hint of blue
tucked securely between the pages
of the journal on the shelf
with the other notebooks on the writing desk
the feather is there to remind me
of the girl, the lake, that day in the Spring
but the feather says
I remember what you do not
I know what you cannot
I know flight

A Birthday Poem

One more trip around the sun
and I am dizzy and lightheaded
from travelling at roller coaster speeds
through empty space and time
my edges burnt to a crisp
my brain, it is sore
from so many years
thinking that I know where I am going
and here I am, right here
back where I started
with the only thing to show
after so many, so very many miles
is an aged body
a little bit rusty
a little slower
and a few more stories to tell

Le Old Navy

I stand in the doorway
as Gabo once stood
very long ago
hungry and broke
but not quite broken
and peer
into the space that is, was
Le Old Navy.

There is Cortázar
at the corner table where he once sat
to the left, writing hard
as if his very hair were on fire.

I turn, walk away
as Marquez once did
and leave so to create a memory
of my own
from their ghosts and anecdotes
of non-existent encounters.

Le Old Navy is exposed now
barren and naked
an empty Parisian bar on Boulevard St. Germaine
in the capital of literature
an empty, soulless vessel.

As these things go,
the pilgrim finds salvation
in the accounts of
the redemption of past pilgrims
who staked our claim
to the calling.

Flower Water
for J.B.

One thousand and twelve black birds
capture youth, only to disappear
this ironic sense of this
and that
assuredly cringe worthy fact
is that their existence varies
like in the exaltation
of flower water.

The kind that brings to a head
retrospect and outliers
as good as any
moniker for Roy Rogers
searching, searching, never finding
the trigger to our disarray.

All of this to say
an appropriate river
can still flow
to an ocean
that has always humbled me
and perhaps, even you.

Honduras

The mountains in the cool mist
lush, green awake under a slowly rising tropical sun
the smell of ancient smoke
cooking fires
and bright colors, flowers, cloth
and birds adorned with rainbows
here amongst the forgotten
rain, pure, hard
comes in waves long enough
to give the sun her *siesta*
for the night is never long enough
to truly cool this earth
where beans and corn
are life
and coffee and bananas
are the crosses born by the poor
and death wears the uniform of a soldier
while the tats on the *norteño* gang children
speak of the unholy love with death's mistresses
dengue and cholera
who wait their turn in the *jacal* down the path
for the mango to turn ripe
for the harvest is near
and the powder white
as the gods of the ancient ones
are to weary to get out of the hammock
to offer a little gift
for the birth of a new day

Lone Star Talking

I am still
that gonzo cosmic cowboy
cool, tall
straight line walking
lone star talking
grace space
one and the same
within, without
that you think you remember
O, so well
from all those years ago
the love child
spawn of the heads
beneath the desert solstice
moon beam
pause for effect
only different

La Brava Corrida

If it's going to be that way
then, so be it
how could it be otherwise
or
why wouldn't you
I don't know
porque no
so said the reluctant *torero*
to the gypsy prostitute
as she practiced her *flamenco* clap
on the cold tile floor
and he prayed
to Our Lady of Pilar
for a clean kill
one where the matador is carried out
prostrate, blood between his thighs
and the bull is awarded
two ears and a tail no less
to thunderous applause
the Sunday after next

Impressionist

For the second time tonight
I heard chitter chatter of angels
black and dark
between her eyes.

Laid to rest
under the flower bed
out back, behind the garden shed
alone but for the sprawling moonlight.

Shadows talking low
give them wide berth
for the calico pony
is forever wanting.

Always in gasps
a woman rinsed in sun
wants yet more
of the thin and bent air
miles too high.

So, is this what is meant
when wedding bells
have been silenced
till dawn.

Sunset

Unless we can measure the distance
between heartbeats
time stands still
and the sun halts just above the horizon
indefinitely.

I hear the symphony
suspended in the mist
of a thousand waves
and I imagine
the patience of silence.

Between heartbeats
you and I float
in an open boat without paddles
on an ocean of memory

In measured rhymes
towards the consolation
of a single sun
suspended in amber
that refuses to set.

The Border Crossing

At the edge of the mesa
under a sun
that knows no nationality
two trails emerge from the distant horizon
through the brush and heat's shimmer
converge at a crossing
on the river, below

Behind me
the land of money on the table
where you just have to show to collect
and there are no trails
only a desert
that swallows families
who disappear
into a fantasy
where the black bear and yellow cactus flower
tell us that water
is a virtue
and to live
is sufficient enough.

Raymond Berthelot is a District Manager with the Louisiana Office of State Parks. Originally from New Orleans, Mr. Berthelot worked in the Archives Department at Xavier University of Louisiana for several years before moving to Baton Rouge. While at Xavier he was the Co-production editor of Xavier Review Press. At Xavier Review Press Mr. Berthelot oversaw the translation of the first works of Honduran poet Marco Tulio del Arca published in the United States, compiled the index to *Chester Himes: An Annotated Primary and Secondary Bibliography*, by Michel Fabre and Robert Skinner, and saw his own short stories and poems published in the pages of *La Prensa*, San Pedro Sula, Honduras. His first nonfiction, "La Fiesta Brava as Art," appeared in *The World of English* (Beijing, China), in an issue that also included an article by Nelson Mandela, during this time.

Mr. Berthelot has gone on to publish several more articles, reviews, and poems, including most recently in the *The Acentos Review, Progenitor Art & Literary Journal, Mantis: A Journal of Poetry, Peregrine Journal, Apricity Magazine, The Elevation Review, Journal of Caribbean Literatures, the Carolina Quarterly, DASH Literary Journal, The Dead Mule, Lothlorien Poetry Journal, The Bluebird Word* and many other diverse literary journals. *The Middle Ages*, Mr. Berthelot's first chapbook of collected poetry, was published in 2022.

Raymond Berthelot holds an M.A. in History from Louisiana State University and two B.A.s, Political Science and History, from the University of New Orleans. Mr. Berthelot is married to Gerardina Berthelot, of La Ceiba, Honduras, and they have one daughter, Oriana. When not travelling, Mr. and Mrs. Berthelot make their home in Baton Rouge, Louisiana, with their two Maltese, Luna Rose and Lily Rose.